# Time Wasted

Camille E. Davis

PAGE PUBLISHING
Conneaut Lake, PA

First originally published by Page Publishing 2023

ISBN 979-8-88654-631-6 (pbk)
ISBN 979-8-88654-632-3 (digital)

Printed in the United States of America

All I want to do is get out of this squad car. How did I get myself into this situation? As I put my head down, I saw the eyes of my daughter with total disappointment. As the police searched my mother's house for a missing gun, my nieces stood and looked at me in handcuffs. The rumor was I took a gun from a neighbor's home. This was all I need.

My mother had been disappointed in me for the past fifteen years. Every time I moved, the handcuffs got tighter and hurt. They had me in front of my mother's home just sitting for hours transferring me from one police car to another. I never thought I wanted to go to jail so quickly just to get off the block. Everybody was looking at me as if I killed someone. All I know is I am embarrassed. All of a sudden, I yelled, "When are you gonna take me into custody?" And after two hours and forty-five minutes, they did.

The police didn't find a gun so they couldn't charge me but took me in because of old bench warrants. I said to myself, "Damn, here I go again." The same routine over and over again, only this time things were a little different. I was a lot older, and I felt scared for the first time, not the kind of scared-for-my-life terrified but fear only God could give me. I just wanted to be booked so I can think. There's too much movement in this sheriff's department. It's too crowded in here, and I remembered thinking, *I wish you nigga's would sit down!* Everyone's talking at the same time, and the sound of everyone's voice started to muffle in my ears. I just wanted to scream, "Shut the hell up!" But I knew if I did I would go to the hole right away, and that's just too much thinking.

After sitting there for hours, they finally booked me. I showered, put on the prison uniform, and went to the assigned dorm. I noticed they were putting two prisoners into a room, but they never gave me a roommate. After a while, I didn't want to be alone. I wanted to joke my time away. I didn't want to feel anymore or think of all the idiotic, pitiful things I've done to people, especially to myself. Not only did I look filthy on the outside, but I was also even dirtier on the inside.

As I sat on the hardest bed in the world, *I started thinking to myself and having heavy flashbacks* of how I ripped the pockets of my neighbor's pants off just to get his wallet. The thread of his pants had to be rotten for them to come off that easily. I flipped him over on his stomach, and the pocket just ripped off. I told him with this crazy look in my eyes, "Don't play with me!"

After two days I thought I was doing him a favor by mailing his wallet back. I started to remember when I robbed two men on the street pretending to be armed. After I robbed them, I rode around in a yellow sports car for hours with drugs and money. Six hours later, there were police, detectives, and patty wagons all around me. I heard them say, "Put your hands up!" I had drugs in my pocket and wasn't going to let them catch me with anything. So I ate eleven bags of powerful crack. I just chewed them up, even the plastic. At the time the police had the nerve to ask me my name. I couldn't talk because the crack had my lips so numb, so I replied, "Cameeba, Cameeba Davis!" They looked at me, shook their heads back and forth, started laughing, and yelled at me to get in the f——ing patty wagon.

I sat in the county jail for months because I got revoked on a previous aggravated battery charge. So while I sat there waiting to be sentenced, I remembered how sad I was, so I started to repent. I remember not eating and fasting most of my time, while other inmates would yell out, "I don't know why you're going to church now. Your ass didn't go when you were out there on the streets." But I just ignored everything they said and kept praying and fasting.

Six months later, I went to court, and I couldn't believe I only got nine months. (*Man, here I go again thinking*). It was too quiet. I needed to get into the population so I can laugh my time away. I still couldn't believe I didn't have a roommate. I needed one because I was thinking too much. Every time I passed this scratched-up mirror, I couldn't even look at myself. And when I think about it, I haven't for some years, when I started to stare, I have to turn away. All I was thinking was I haven't been in trouble since the *aggravated battery* and that I was too old to be in custody with all these younger thugs. So I turn away from the scratched-up mirror quickly, and as I glanced at myself in the mirror, I just didn't like what I see. *So I yelled out*, "When am I going to court? I'm only here on a bench warrant!" But they were not paying me any attention, so I started to lie down. Maybe I could sleep this time away.

As I placed my head on the rough pillow, *I start to remember* the day I was so high, and now that I think about it, someone had to slip me a mickey, or maybe I just was on crack too many days. I was so hot with heat. I took off my leather coat, and all I had on was my bra. How I didn't get hit by a car was beyond me. Because I was walking down the busiest street in Milwaukee, Wisconsin, I pulled the fire alarm to save my own life unconsciously. I was told that I knocked on this woman's door, looked through her glass door window while she was holding her own baby, and thought she stole the baby. Of course, she called the police.

The police put me in jail overnight just like the town drunk on *Andy Griffith*, and they let me go the next morning. The police asked my mother, "Does your daughter have a mental problem?" Upon release, I was told all I did was spit and laugh during my whole time in the squad car. My mother let me call a cab home, and when I walked into the house, you could hear a pin drop. I felt so stupid that when I got in the house, I didn't say nothing to nobody. A couple of days later, the remorseful feeling did not last. Before I knew anything, I started acting crazy again.

That same day, I went to the store and saw this man stuff a big wad of money in his front right pocket. All I knew was I had to have this money. I got on the same side where he put that wad of money, and *one, two, three*, I shoved my hand down his pocket and came up with all those hundreds of dollars. I ran like Wilma Rudolph down alleys, backyards, and between houses, until I got to Atkinson Street. After that, I had to get high. I smoked so fast because of what I did. I found myself looking out windows, blinds, keyholes, and even nail holes in the walls.

I asked anybody and everyone to get high with me because I didn't like to get high by myself. But when the dope was gone, I got so mad at the people who helped me smoke. I'd tell them to go rob somebody I especially liked and couldn't wait for any one of them to brag on themselves saying, "Baby girl, you know I have a heart!" That's just what I needed to hear because now I wanted you to prove it! I would say to them. "Go prove it. Get some money!" By the time I finished trying to convince them, they would look at me saying, "Camille, you crazy," and they would leave. While backing their way out of my sight I thought to myself, *They weren't so nuts after all.*

The things I did to stay high were walking into folks' houses and throwing their DVDs, TVs, and VCRs in the pillowcases out the window into the snowbanks. Then I would get high with them, and they would actually look puzzled, shaking their heads back and forth saying to themselves, "Camille couldn't have done it because she was here the whole time." I remember the days when I would walk up and down streets looking for victims, always speaking to people hoping once I would get them in a conversation. I knew I had them right where I wanted them.

A few months went by, and I found myself still doing the same things, only this time I got a job. Welding was my occupation, and I was very good at it. I graduated from Airco Technical Institute in Chicago, Illinois, in 1987, so getting a job was never a problem, but keeping one was. As the years went by, I remember drinking more heavily than ever before. I was invited to several parties and different taverns. There was one bar in particular that I found to be very interesting, only because it was 90 percent women, and I was there every weekend.

Years went by, I found myself chasing women in gay taverns and going to private parties, until five and seven in the morning. That was the time I should have been at work. I was wasting my time with worthless women who really didn't know what they wanted. I was thinking they wanted to be in this gay relationship, and we would live together like a man and a woman would live. When I come home, my food better be cooked and my work clothes better be clean. As I thought about everything now, all the three long-term relationships I had with these women just got out of long commitments with men. All three women ended up being the same—sexy and promiscuous.

It really started off great in the beginning. Then when they realized *Camille is serious, and she really wants a real relationship*, they started to say to themselves, "Maybe I was not cut out for this lifestyle after all." It only took a year or two before they left me. Plus, I know I was not the easiest person to live with. I became too serious and abusive in every way. And naturally, when my relationship ended, I went back home to my mother's house.

My poor mother just didn't know where she went wrong. I'm sure she asked herself, "Lord, why is my daughter with women?" I was trying to even think to myself, *how did I get this way*? It just happened that I knew as a young girl I liked women, and I hated myself for it. I was confused and did not know how to relate to men growing up. They made me uncomfortable. I didn't have too many male figures in my life, and the one I had was very sarcastic and often belittling, so my impression of men was not that hot.

I was born in Waukesha, Wisconsin. I was the youngest out of four. It was my brother who was a navy man, my two sisters, then myself. My father had an asphalt business and was the first Black counselor at the Wells boys' home. My mother met my father while he was in the army, and they married, and she became a homemaker. Before my mother met my father, she was born and raised in Bloomington, Illinois. My mother was raised by her grandmother, Lucy. Lucy was well known to all the people in that town. When anyone would come into town, and you didn't have anything, people would go to her, and she would feed you and give you food to take home. She grew her vegetables herself and canned what they would call piccalilli and other healthy things.

Lucy and my mother's uncles, Homer and Torrence, who were police officers in Joliette, Illinois, loved my mother, and they cherished and adored my mom, so being spoiled was an understatement. Now my mother raised me in a Pentecostal Church in Waukesha, Wisconsin, where my godgrandmother was the pastor, Rev. Gertrude E. Vonner. The saints and the mothers of the church taught us how to reach God for ourselves at the altar. And every Sunday, my godcousins would laugh because when they had an altar call, I would be the first person running up there.

The older saints would make me repeat after them by saying, "Tell the Lord, 'Save me.' Tell the Lord you love Him, and tell the Lord, 'Forgive me,' over and over again." It never failed as a child in my early years I had since enough to know that the altar was for the saints as well as the sinner. I always knew there was something I had to repent for.

So I made sure before I left Sunday service, my slate was wiped clean. I guess I just had to have that reassurance.

When I got older, I'm sure my mother questioned why my life was like it was, but she showed me lots of love anyway. How my life got this out of hand is beyond me. My mother was a very attractive woman, very wise, and very tactful. She always carried herself with class. She was elegant, graceful, well-spoken, very funny, and had a great sense of humor. My mom was the kind of mother who would kick in a door to rescue her children if she knew we were doing anything to degrade ourselves, especially if she knew where we were. My father on the other hand was a family man but very much a drinker, outspoken, handsome, macho, and bold. He had a business mind and always knew how to make thousands of dollars.

At a young age, my parents legally separated, and we moved to Milwaukee, Wisconsin. A few years down the road, my mother met our stepfather. We moved to 36 Hampton Avenue. My stepfather was a wonderful man. He was White, so a lot of times people would make certain comments. But it didn't bother us girls. We were proud and very happy. Even though he wasn't emotional, he was a great provider; we didn't want for anything. I'll always cherish our childhood memories of going to Dandelion Park in Muskego, Wisconsin. We went just about every weekend.

I don't think my stepfather ever missed a day at work. He was a cool cat. As a young girl playing outside, I met my first friend. Her name was Erie Crowder. Her daughter and I were close in age, so we often rode our bikes together and jumped rope. But Mrs. Crowder always made me feel special. I remembered my first real crush was her son, Michael.

We called him Big Man. As a young girl, I thought he was the dreamiest I had ever seen. So of course I stayed across the street, just to see him.

Mrs. Crowder always made me feel like I was so humorous, always laughing with me. She made me feel so included in their family. I just felt like a crowder after a while. LOL. I remembered introducing my mother to her, and they became best friends. Inseparable. It was like watching Ethel and Lucy, Thelma and Louise in the shopping malls. They were like sisters. Mrs. Crowder was not opposed to giving me a spanking if I got out of line. I guess I got comfortable with her and started calling her by her first name, Erie. And because that was a form of disrespect, before I even crossed the street, my mother was waiting for me on our porch with this you're-gonna-get-it look.

My sister, Cozette, was the sister who always had the family BBQs and great gatherings at her home. She was a great host and would make anyone welcome. Very friendly. I remember Cozette was always listening to Chaka Khan and actually singing like her. She knew all the lyrics and made it easy for me to fall in love with Chaka Khan too. But her favorite music was rock 'n' roll. She was a great artist and could draw and paint just about anything. She loved to dress and could put on her makeup like a model, a very generous person, not to mention the most beautiful of all three of us sisters.

Now my oldest sister Chauncey was really easy to talk to with a skin tone that was high yellow. Her personality was a lot more groovy than most. I grew up listening to her loving the Ohio Players and Bootsy Collins, but her favorite was rock 'n' roll. She was the only person I ever met who can have all her ex-mates in one room, and they were trying to get along so they don't get kicked out just to be around her. WOW. If anybody messed with me, she'd be the first person to come to my rescue, ready to beat the world for me, with her little self. I always admired how she could keep such loyal and good friends, then one day, she just told me, "Camille, if you want friends, you need to be friendly. It's just that simple."

My brother Lyle, who's the oldest, is a very handsome man who went to the Navy and always put me in the mind of a person who always demanded respect. His favorite music is rock 'n' roll, and I remembered him always playing the Delfonics. He is a great artist and could draw anything. I remember a spooky picture he made; it was a clown, and the clown's eyes would look at you anywhere in the house you stood. I got rid of that piece of art.

I always felt I bothered my brother because he seemed aggravated when I came around. But as I got older, I tried my best to think why I annoyed him so much. Maybe I was just an aggravating kid growing up. Not to mention when he realized I became a lesbian drug addict and criminal that really did it. How embarrassing. Nevertheless, I adore my big brother. He is and will always be the most handsome, macho man I'll ever meet, and I'm always proud to say that's my brother.

Years went by and one afternoon, Chauncey took me out. I believe she took me out just to ask if I was a lesbian; as the night went on, she got her answer and politely told Mom, "It's not a phase." My mom, being so strong, kept a lot of hurt inside. She always told me, "Camille, if you're going to have that lifestyle, be sharp, dress nice, stay clean, be a decent person in life, but most of all give God time, He knows your heart."

I think no one knew how I felt. Mostly it was embarrassing because during all my relationships, I was always so puffed up. I thought I had it going on because all my women were so beautiful and had money. And now that it was gone, all I have left is alcohol, so I'll go out tonight. I don't want to think about how I messed up these friendships with these three women. I drank so much during that entire month. I found myself using heavier drugs, like powdered cocaine and crack, I even started snorting China white.

After that experience, it was time for me to get some serious help. I realized it wasn't so cool walking around with my eyes closed and still telling people I know where it was. After that, I decided to go into treatment. I heard of this place called April House, so I went in for help. That following week I started an inpatient program. After several months of treatment, I decided to go to an outside meeting. That was when I met this nice man.

He was a lot older than me, but because of his conversation, he caught my attention. He was an employee of Harley Davidson for several years. He and I talked for hours, and I found out he was at the meeting because of a drinking problem. After the meeting was over, I could tell he was very fond of me. What got my attention was his great-paying job. So after spending a lot of time talking to him, he would call me on several occasions to pick him up and take him all around on business. What I liked most about him was when he gave me something; he wasn't cheap, and he always made me feel like I was the only woman in the room. I never had to question how much he adored me. He and I could never really get together like we wanted to because of our living situation. But soon, my time here will be completed, and I'll be home.

I would think after six months of intense treatment, I'd be okay, but I really want to tie one on today. The same day I left treatment, he called me to pick him up. When I arrived, he was already drinking. I had never ever seen anybody in my entire life drink a bottle of vodka straight down before, just like a glass of water. After sitting in total silence, I started to realize he didn't want to go back to the facility. He seemed so stressed so I sat with him for a minute, got some money from him, and dropped him off. One thing I admired about him was he never missed a day of work. He was nothing like me. He was totally functional when it came to his job.

I continued seeing him for a couple of years until one evening, he told me his mother was going out of town to visit family. So he asked me if I would like to spend the night. That evening we had such a great time. We ate real good, we drank, and we laughed, but most of all we talked like never before and started to hold each other all night. I looked at him for the first time and started to appreciate the kind of real man he was inside. He was kind and always had a good word to say. Even though I was really rough around the edges, he still loved me anyway, and I didn't want anything. The same night, we had sex, and all I could think about was how the bed kept squeaking over, and over, and over again driving me crazy to the point I told him, "Wake me when you're through." The next morning I showered and went home.

The following weekend, a couple of friends asked me out on the town. There was a new gay bar that just opened up, and I had to show off I just got a new outfit. We had so many shots of tequila with beer chasers and danced the night away. I couldn't even remember what time I got home, but when I woke up, I had the sickest feeling I ever had. I started to throw up. But this just wasn't any kind of illness. It was a violent vomit. It was as if the vomit was coming from my big toe. I regurgitated all my body acids from within.

At that point, I knew my crazy butt was pregnant. All I could say to myself was bad timing. I just got out of a relationship with this woman, and I would be laughed at by everyone I know, not to mention I liked this other woman I just met. I began to wonder what I was going to do and what my friends were going to say about me. I was supposed to be a stud. How was I going to look? Walking around with a big stomach being such a butchy-acting woman. It wasn't gonna look right! How do I explain this mess?

After crying all that night, the next day, I got the pregnancy confirmed at planned parenthood. The nurse came into the patient room and told me, "Yes, Camille, you're going to have a baby." As I walked out of the office, I couldn't wait to get home so I could call him on the phone, and when I told him, all he had to say was, "I'm too old to have a baby. My family's going to think I'm crazy!" After all that, I was glad we were on the same page.

A week later he gave me abortion money, but before I knew anything, I spent it on an outfit I liked at the Grand Avenue Mall. I told myself I have time, and I was not showing yet. When I talked to him later that evening, I told him I spent the money and needed more. This time he was smart enough to give the money to my mother, but eventually, I got a hold of that too. I really wasn't ready to face anything at the time and continued to party.

As the weeks went by, I started to feel sluggish so I went to a regular doctor and got some prenatal vitamins. When I got home from the doctor's office, I started to feel embarrassed and mad at myself. I sat at the table and started to cry. I cried so hard that all of the blood vessels in my eyes broke. I looked awful, but most of all, I was very ashamed of myself. I finally got up from the kitchen table and started to brush my teeth, wash my face, and change my clothes. The doorbell rang, and I peeked out of the window, and it was this woman I met through my ex-girlfriend. Now this woman was the most beautiful woman I had ever seen, and when she walked, all heads turned, even straight women's. Her hair was dark red but very long and stylish. Her skin was a sexy bronze color because she tanned easily. When I first saw her, I thought she was Greek or Italian.

To make a long story short, she was drop-dead gorgeous with her sharp clothes and sports car. Before I even opened the door, I tried to fix myself up but knew I had to hurry up before she left. As I opened the door, the aroma of her fragrance put me at ease. We sat at the kitchen table. She had this smile on her face. I couldn't quite understand why she had that look on her face. A few seconds later she said, "Camille, how are you?" I replied, "Fine, how about you?" Then all of a sudden she came out and said, "Camille, are you pregnant?" All I could say was, "Yes." I started to put my head in my hands, and she held onto my arms.

How she knew I was pregnant was beyond me, but I forgot I had my prenatal vitamins on the table. And all of a sudden I started to cry. As she held me, she asked me what I was going to do. I yelled out, "What do you mean what I'm I going to do. I'm going to have an abortion!" I began to tell her I can't walk around with my stomach big. My friends were going to laugh at me! I was supposed to be a stud. How was I going to face people like this? I'll be the laughing joke of everything. I'm butch. I'll look ridiculous. All of a sudden, silence filled the room.

She turned and looked deep into my eyes and said, "Camille, you're still a woman. Keep the baby." And it was that very moment I started to feel not so alone. Someone was actually there for me. She got me to leave the house, and she took me out to eat. Two weeks later, she put a tattoo of my name really fancy on her right breast, and yes I thought I was the shit. And before I knew anything, hours, days, and years went by, and my daughter was now two years old. My friend named my daughter Simone, only I decided to spell it S-A-M-O-N-E.

My friend and I decided to take it to the next level and move in together. After meeting her mother, we decided to move in. Her mother didn't seem to mind, besides her home was so huge she never saw or heard us anyway. One thing about her family was that they loved cats, and at the time, she had a cat named Spiky, and her mother had a cat named China. She even went a step further and got Samone a cat, and we named it Mousey because it was gray and looked like a mouse.

The cat and my daughter were the same age, and as they both grew up together, I started noticing she pulled on the cat so much until the cat was actually bald. It didn't matter to Mousey. He loved her so. The cat was so overprotective of my daughter. If he never met you before, he would give you a hard time. One day my older sister decided to sit down on one of the wicker chairs. The cat went around the back of the chair and dug his claws deep through the wicker and into her back. All I could see was my sister running around with a cat and a chair on her back screaming.

As the day went by, I started to realize this friend helped me in so many ways. She saved me from so much hurt because I had just gotten out of a relationship. And while I was dealing with the unexpected pregnancy, it seemed like she came into my life right when I needed her. It wasn't hard to fall for her right away because of her loving nature and good looks. This one particular evening, we were laughing as usual. She began to tell me about her drug use before she met me. She began to tell me she had been clean for a number of years. She continued to commend herself on how she changed her friends and how proud she was of all her success in life lately, with her brand new sports car, and the trust back with family members. She went on to say how much she was starting to love herself again. We ended the conversation with a laugh when she mentioned her cat Spiky never came by her when she was high.

While she was talking, I hated myself because I started visualizing us getting high together. That following weekend, we asked her mother if she would watch Samone, and we went out for drinks. She didn't even want to drink, but I pressured her so much until she ordered a rum and coke. After several drinks, I knew in my mind exactly where we were going—straight to the dope house. She didn't know or even want to, but as soon as I pulled up to the dope house, she was pissed off. She told me, "I thought we were going home!" So I simply turned to her and said, "I need a hit." And in my mind, I knew it was a bad idea, but at that time, the drug was more important. Besides, with all the alcohol I consumed, I couldn't talk myself out of this situation if I wanted to. The dealers of the household were so glad to see us of course. We had lots of money. So we got the royal treatment.

As I ordered, I saw my friend looking at me. So I was starting to feel guilty. I told the dope man to hurry up with my order, knowing with every inhale of this good crack, the look my girl was giving me won't mean anything. As a matter of fact, I knew it was just a matter of time before she'll be asking me to pass her a pipe and light her up. Before I knew anything, several hours went by, and we were out of money. I remembered us sitting at the dirty scratched-up table looking sideways to see if I still had some dope left on the table. I recalled sweating a lot, and my hands and fingers were black because of the filthy pipe. As my eyes bulged out of my head, I asked the dope man for credit. I said, "Hey man, I spent a lot of money. Can I get a couple of bags on credit?" He looked at me for a long time as if I was talking in another language. But after I got done talking, and talking, he finally gave it to me. We left and took those few bags home.

While driving back home, I felt all communication was totally gone between her and me. A few years went by, and Samone was now five years old. We moved into a house on West Capitol Drive. It was great for us because we had something of our own. We never ever displayed any sexual, lustful attention toward each other in front of my daughter. But we found ourselves getting high almost every day. The more I got high, the more my friend hated me. It only took a couple of months before all the beautiful custom diamond rings that she had specially made for me were on the fingers of dope dealers' wives. Every time she would look at me, I could see the hate in her eyes. Our relationship turned from adoring each other to not wanting to be in the same room with each other.

This went on for another year 'till one day I had this weird feeling. It was so strange, but it had to do with one or both of my sisters. That morning I stayed very quiet. I told my friend I knew something was going to happen. I didn't quite know what it was. I just knew something felt very wrong. A week later I was watching the news, and while watching, they had a familiar part of town roped off. The anchorwoman said, "Police are looking for a suspect in a shooting, one man dead, and one female in critical condition, both shot in the head." All I knew was I couldn't sleep.

Two hours later, my mother called me on the phone, and when I saw the time, and how late it was, I couldn't bear to hear what my mother had to say to me. I recalled shaking as she talked, and she told me my sister Cozette got shot in the head. She was a gunshot victim in 1994 who was just sitting in a car with her friend in the parking lot of Walgreens on Third and North Avenue. When my mother and I hung up the phone, all I could do was run out of the house. When I got to the hospital, I went into the room where my sister was. All I could see was her long cascading hair that had to be shaved completely off so they could find the entry of the bullet and drain most of the pressure off the brain or something. I didn't quite know.

As I was looking at my beautiful sister, I noticed her eyes were half-opened. I tried to bend down far enough so maybe she could see me. While looking at her, I felt there was no life at all, and for the very first time in my entire life, I can honestly say my heart was broken. Nine days later, Cozette died. We buried her on September 22, 1994. My poor mother. I had never seen such a brave woman before in all my life. She was so strong. She sang songs along with the people at the funeral. But what I admired about my mother the most was how she greeted the people who paid their respects. She smiled through it all.

When the funeral was over, I remember my mother falling flat on her face toward her pillow. I didn't have to hear her cry but felt the hurt with every body movement she made. And when I looked at her it, was as if the world had come to an end. All of a sudden I heard a deep whimpering. It was all over, and she knew she would never ever see her daughter Cozette again. I knew at this point even I couldn't help. It was between her and God. I felt so bitter.

All I remembered was me and my girlfriend, Wendy, arguing each day. It got to the point we started throwing knives at one another until I got tired and started using my fist. After the fight, I thought I would go take a shower, and when I got out of the shower, I got taken out by the police. They had the nerve to handcuff me naked. I got arrested for domestic violence. This went on between her and me for years. I've been getting arrested for OWI and driving after revocation. So the next time I got police contact, they decided to put me in the house of correction for six months.

After court, they put the handcuffs on me, and they took me straight into custody. They charged me for being a habitual traffic offender. After being at the HOC for three months, I finally got by a phone. I called home, and Wendy told me my mother came over and straight-up took my daughter out of the house. She said all she could do was cry and look stupid. My mother took over, and there was nothing she could do about it. My mother never took custody of my daughter, but she did all the necessary things you're supposed to do for a child when you're taking care of them, like keeping them in a healthy environment, teaching my daughter about the love of God, and showing her how to respect herself.

And believe it or not, I was very happy Samone was with my mother. I knew I would be in jail for a while, and my mother's home was the healthiest place for her. In jail, I was known for being crazy. But most of all, I was known for being a leader. Some deputies even looked at me as the person most likely to incite a riot, only because prisoners liked and listened to me so much. So a lot of the time they would watch me; they knew I could get the inmates' participation to do most anything.

During my time in jail, I always went to Bible study. I went because I had since enough to know God sat me down again to get my attention. I just couldn't see myself sitting down in this dorm talking to the Lord in silence. I was compelled to worship, with praises, clapping, and singing. I needed a breakthrough. I knew I wanted to get close to Him that night, and the only way that was going to happen I had to lift the name of Jesus. I wasn't ashamed to worship the Lord in front of other prisoners. So when Bible study was called, I hurried up at the chance to sign my name.

As I entered the room where we had the study, there was this White woman standing there looking at me as I entered. Before I got a chance to sit down, she said to me, really loud, "You think you're all that and a bag of chips!" And she continued, "Yes you!" After that, all I could hear was silence in the room. I continued to sit down, and this White woman began to talk with so much power, and all I could do was sit on the edge of my seat.

Everything she uttered was for me, and she seemed to only be speaking to me. During her powerful, anointed preaching, she would stop, look over at me, and say, "God had a calling on my life that I was very special to Him, and God was going to use me in a mighty way." She continued then she turned to me again and asked me my name. After the Bible study was over, I had to know this woman's name. She started to hug me and began speaking in tongues. When she looked at me, it was as if she could look right through me. For the first time in a long time, someone saw something worthwhile in me.

As I walked back to the dorm I was quiet the whole way back. People I used to laugh with were wondering why I was so quiet. Things weren't the same, I just didn't feel like joking around so much. I had such a peace within that when I got back to the dorm, my attitude was totally different. That night I lay on my bunk just meditating on what this woman preached about.

At 1:00 a.m., I had to use the bathroom. After urinating, I got off the toilet and went over to wash my hands. As I was looking at my hands while washing, I started to look around. My eyes went from looking at myself in the mirror to looking at the showers. All of a sudden, I needed to start writing. I knew I had to be very quiet because this deputy who was on duty was no joke. She'll put you in the hole for dropping a pencil, so I knew I had to be very quiet. I got my paper out and grabbed my pencil, and without a doubt, *I knew the Lord wanted me to write* about what I was feeling at that moment. When I started writing, it was non-stop. I found myself erasing one or two lines but finished a whole page within five minutes. It was as if I was possessed. This is what the Lord had me write:

Showers, freedom, dinner, where's my mail?
Sometimes I feel like I ended in hell.
I need answers, where's my visit, my phone call in all
Waiting to hear I've taken a fall.
Life, Camille, you're a loser, you know you're the blame.
Don't you know your daughter Samone is ashamed?
Hey, you were out, you decided to play,
Now that you're caught, "Oh god," you say!
You thought you had it good.
You treat your family bad,
Knowing all the time there, all you have.
Going out, partying, drinking, doing drugs.
Hanging all night on the corner with those thugs.
Some of them stand with their hands filled with blood.
Disrespecting yourself all through the night.
Not even caring if it was your last flight.

Putting your family in all kinds of danger
Running around like you're the lone ranger
Thank God for His mercy, thank God for His grace.
Someone had to put you back into your place
You still got to pay for what you've done
You broke man's law, so put away the gun
And even though your life was fading,
God almighty was always waiting.

After writing those words, I started to see how stupid I was acting. I got excited because I was grateful God was talking to me again, showing me myself, but most of all how disrespectful I had become. God was actually letting me see myself on paper, but He was also showing me my gift. I decided to recite my testimonial poem to everyone and anybody who would listen. Some cried, some stayed quiet, and some talked about me, saying how could I talk about myself like that. But all I could do was walk away smiling. The Bible study was tonight, and I can't wait to recite my poem to the White woman who spoke powerful anointed words that seemed to be speaking only to me.

As I walked into the Bible study, our eyes connected right away. It was as if we were friends. I was happy to see her, and she seemed happy to see me. I quickly asked her if I could do a poem. After saying my poem, she looked at me, the look on her face and in her eyes, anyone could see she was in the spirit. When the study was over, she started to tell me things about myself only God and I knew. The Bible study was just about over, and we all had to go back to the dorm, so I quickly asked her, "What's your name?" She replied, "Cheryl Wilks." She quickly gave me her address so I could write to her. She was a hard woman to converse with because all the prisoners needed her spirit to give advice. Everyone wanted to talk to her, and she always had a great crowd around her.

As we all walked back to the dorm, right before I could even get into the doorway, *I heard a whisper in my inner ear.* What I heard was "Abomination." Well, I had enough since to know the Lord wanted me to write. I said to myself, "Camille, if you had to write about this word, what would you come up with?" So I started thinking about different people in the neighborhood who were pointing their fingers at me, saying things like, "She's gay, laughing, at me as I walk to the store." They already knew my name is Camille but decided to call me everything else. As I was walking, they shouted out things such as:

Abomination

"Hey, Tommy. Hey, Henry. Hey, Jimmy. Hey, Fred!"
Girl, what's your name?" "It's Camille," I said.
"Well, how would we know. You look so content."
"Girl, what's that smell!"
"Why do you look so masculine?"
"In the Bible, it says Adam and Eve,
And by the way, you look Camille,
I swear you were Steve,
If your mama could see you
I'm sure she would grieve!"
*Do you think I can help the way I feel?*
*You act as if I can take a pill.*
I didn't get this overnight,

So you and your friend can stop calling me a dyke.
God almighty died for my sins,
All I gotta do is learn to give in,
And if I call on His name,
He'll wash me in His blood,
And if I never turn back,
He'll act as if it's never been done.
I know God's will; this is not my station.
And I know the Holy Bible. It's an *abomination*!
But I've been this way all my life,
My thoughts should have changed. I
should have been a man's wife.
Wasting all my time, sleeping with,
Wendy, Susan, and Pam,
When Jesus was standing by my side,
Saying, "Camille, here I *am*!"
Lord, help me, I can't change this lifestyle by myself.
Where did Camille go?
Did I put her on a shelf?
The Lord said:
*"Camille's right here. Let me bring her out! And*
*when I do, Camille, I mean you better*
*shout! For I am the life, the truth, and*
*The way. Rebuke the devil when he says*
*you're gay!"*

After I finished, God showed me how hurt I was by
this crazy lifestyle. He showed me through this very poem
that if I would rebuke the devil, I didn't have to live this
way anymore. I couldn't wait to recite this poem to everyone. It didn't matter to me, the inmates, the sergeant, the

deputies. It just didn't matter. God showed me my gift, and I wanted to share it with everyone.

In a couple of days, Sister Cheryl Wilks will be coming to do Bible study, and I couldn't wait to do my poem for her. I felt like a kid, and everyone was looking at me like one. Every time I would walk around people, they just knew I wanted to say my poems. I remember inmates looking at me with big disappointment; some looked at me with hate, and some walked away saying, "She's stupid for talking about herself like that." But most of them stayed away from me because the rumor was I was degrading myself.

Later on that night, I realized the poems made them feel guilty. I wasn't only talking about me; I was talking about them. When I walked around them, they became very quiet. Conviction had set in on some of the inmates, and they left me completely alone. But when I read my poems, I was on a high only the Lord could bring me down from this, only because God was talking to me again, and I could actually hear Him. As I smiled that entire evening, I fell into a deep sleep.

Around three in the morning, I woke up all of a sudden and couldn't get back to sleep. It didn't take a long time to figure out that the Lord wanted me to grab my pencil and paper, so finally I did, and these were the words the good lord had me write about myself again.

If it wasn't for you, Lord,
I know I will be dead
Walking down dark alleys
Trying to steal somebody's bread.

I've belittled myself once too often,
I'm surprised I've never ended up in a coffin.
God gave me some food, clothes, and a job I take
my will back, and now I look like a slob.
My daughter was so excited,
She thought her mama was going to make it.
I didn't have the decency to even try and fake it.
What's the point of holding money, Camille?
It doesn't do you any good.
You always say what you're going to
buy, but it ends up in the hood.
Now you walk around in circles
Trying to make some kind of sense,
And all the time God's watching
As He has to smell your stench,
God gave me my daughter,
To love, honor, and rise,
So everything wrong in life she does,
Will only be a phase.

When I finished those words, all I did was cry. I think I cried all that morning because when it was time to get up for breakfast, people were asking me if I was alright.

All I could say to them was God revealed a little more about me through another poem. Of course, they quickly walked away. And even though I might have had a sad look on my face, I was grateful. So that's why I decided to name that poem "Grateful." By this time, captains heard about my poems. They would come into the dorm and ask me if I could recite. I loved to say my poems because I didn't need the paper. They were my testimonial poems, so of course,

I knew them by heart. So I would definitely put more dramatics and flair into the reciting.

After all the excitement throughout the weeks, I called my mother's house. When I heard my mother accepted my phone call, she sounded as if something was wrong. She asked me if I was sitting down, and I told her, no, and quickly I asked her, "What's wrong?" My mother sadly told me my girlfriend of seven years, the one who named my daughter, the one who loved me when I didn't love myself, the one who still wanted me even when I was pregnant, had died, and her son found her in her bed lifeless. To this day I still don't know if it was a suicide, or maybe she just put too much heroin in the needle. Nevertheless, she's gone, and all I can do is painfully hang up the phone.

I can't believe the woman who stood by me and helped me through the roughest time of my life was dead, the only person who helped take the embarrassment away when I was at my lowest point was gone. How could this be? I asked the deputy if they could put me in the hole. I just didn't want to be in the population. I can't even get out for her funeral. That entire month was terrible for me. I didn't say too much to anyone, and while sitting in jail, I got fatter than ever. I decided to be a pod worker, hoping I could get an early release. I mopped the bathrooms and kept the dorm room clean every night. After doing that for a month, I decided to write to the captain, and in two weeks, they released me. I finally was out on the streets.

It didn't take long for me to forget everything God had revealed to me about my life through my testimonial poems. All those words of warning went right out the window. I partied like I was going off to college. I found a new circle of friends, and they had more money and could keep me higher longer. I thought I had it going on. Most of the time I would get the things my daughter needed and basically smoke up the rest. Then there were times I knew my mother and my daughter didn't really need anything, so I would spend my whole check on drugs and alcohol not even thinking of my family at all.

I would be out for days, with the same clothes on. If I was on a mission and didn't want to go home, I would wash my face in a tavern bathroom and use soap and water to brush and comb my hair back. I usually had lipstick and eyeliner, and if I went to the next house, I would get high, and I would steal it out of the bathroom cabinet. People knew if they saw me out, I either had drugs or money. I just wouldn't be out trying to get something. If I didn't have it, my butt would be home asleep. Folks knew I was going to get mine by any means necessary. That was probably how I got the nickname Hurricane Camille. I was wild, and I'd get anyone high that was around me, but you better be able to come up with a plan to get more.

It seemed like on every mission I was in, I was degrading myself more and more. It got to the point where nobody trusted me. Even when I had money, dope dealers didn't want to be bothered with me. They knew when my money would run out. I could talk them out of big credit. Most of the time I would pay it back. But sometimes I was late. Being geeked and hiding from dangerous dope dealers wasn't enjoyable. It had you looking and walking around like you're crazy and out of your mind with a mad fear. When people would run into you, you would always look crazy in their eyes.

I've had five brand new cars from Toyota's lot three repossessed and two totaled. All three credit reports were in the four hundred, and hoping to find a trick along the way, a car always stops for my crazy butt, and if one does, they better have a lot of dope or lots of money. Hopefully, they'll drop their wallet. I found myself walking for miles just to get a rock smaller than my baby fingernail.

In my mind, I really didn't feel like anything physical that night. Actually, that night reminded me of the time I went to this bar on Fond Du Lac Avenue. I ordered my usual tequila and beer chaser. I began to laugh at this young man who lost his pool game. Before I knew anything, he politely went to where I was sitting and hit me in the head with the wider side of the pool stick really hard. All I could do was stand there, and I asked him to please not hit me again as the blood ran down my face. I finished my drinks and got my change from the $20 bill, and I walked out. I wiped the blood off of my hair and face. I left as people laughed, and I continued to party.

Everywhere I went, people at other taverns threatened to cut me off because they thought I was drunk. I kept falling down in the tavern. Little did they know, it was the blow to my head, because I had a concussion. They kept yelling out things like, "Look at her!" and in the back of my mind, I knew what was still going on. I even knew I looked ridiculous. Finally, when I got home on the third day, my family already knew I got hit with a pool stick. How they knew was beyond me.

When my sister Chauncey saw my head, she convinced me to go to the doctor. So the next day, the nurse cleaned and stitched me up. I got some great pain pills and went home. I was lucky they were able to stitch me up after four days. When all that was over, I decided to cool down for a few months. As I sat around my mother's house, I started to feel very depressed. I started to feel very lonely, very unattractive, unloved, hated, and anything but worthy. I began to think of my woman, my good friend, who passed away, who stuck beside me through all those years, and all the other relationships I had that failed. I began to blame them for my unhappiness.

When I look at everyone else smiling and going on with their lives, I felt I wasn't good enough to get anyone (man or woman). I wanted something but didn't know what. All I knew is I wanted to be happy. I saw my daughter looking at me crazy, and my mind was telling me she heard other family members talking about me behind my back. I really couldn't be too upset because I was something to talk about. Damn, where did Camille go?

I realized I'd been beating myself up for three months. It was time for me to hit some taverns tonight. After five or six shots of tequila and a pitcher of beer, I may even start liking myself a little more. As the night went on, I hoped someone drops some money. I could use a blast tonight. I saw the dope man come into the tavern, and I felt very excited all of a sudden. It was a crazy night because one of my old friends whom I haven't seen in ages popped into the bar. He and I used to run together back in the eighties. He had more hustle than anybody I knew. I had tall respect for him because he kept us high with no money at all. I just hated to keep driving around. I was the only one who knew how to drive a stick shift at the time.

When those dealers saw him and me coming, he talked to them for a few minutes and came back with money and drugs. When we made eye contact, old times flashed before our eyes, and once again we hung out like old times. He had a godmother who sold crack, so we went over to her house to see what we could get. When I found out the woman sold dope, she became so attractive to me. I made it my business to get acquainted with her, and one thing led to another.

After I talked to her on the porch for several hours, I started to see she was attracted to me. She stopped running in and out of the house anymore to do business. She sat with me for long periods of time. I knew that was very rare for her. She started giving me lots of compliments on my big beautiful eyes, and after she kept looking at me for so long, I knew it was only a matter of time before she would invite me into her house. My ego was so built up that all I could think about was crack. She didn't get high but continued to give me what I wanted. I didn't mind getting high around her. She made me feel very at ease. Plus I knew if I wanted more, I'd better be cool.

I started to look at her real good for the first time, and when I did, I noticed a very good-looking, older woman. She made me feel like she had never been with a woman before. But as the months rolled around, I knew better. I loved the fact that she fell asleep easily. She took pills she said for her back, and when she went to sleep, I would take advantage of all the drugs I wanted. I just hated getting high by myself so I would get high with her daughter and her brother downstairs. When I thought she was about to wake up, I'd sneak upstairs, looking really crazy. She would say, "Camille, what's wrong with you?" All I could do was stare at her as if my eyes were coming out of my head.

After six months of doing the same routine, she got tired of me, so she had her nephew beat me up really bad. I mean the young man hit me like he was Sugar Ray Leonard. With every punch, my whole body turned. He hit me so many times in the middle of the street that his grandmother yelled out, "Stop hitting that girl like that!" I thanked God for his grandmother. The very last thing I remembered him saying to me was, "Don't come back to her anymore!" and pointed a gun in my face so I left, and never came back. When we parted ways, I didn't go home right away. I tried to get high some more, but everywhere I went, dope dealers and crackheads didn't even want to get high with me or even sell me anything, and I had plenty of money. I had so much pain in my face. I decided to take my pathetic butt home.

When I walked into my mother's home once again, my entire family knew I got beat up. I looked at myself in the mirror, and I couldn't believe what I saw. My face looked like Mike Tyson hit me. My lips were split open; my jaw looked fractured. My nose looked and felt broken. My whole face was crooked, and I looked unrecognizable. My daughter was so glad I was home. She came into my room, and when she saw my face, I could see the hurt in her eyes. My daughter was so heartbroken; all I could see were tears coming down her face. She quickly walked away, and I began to cry. At that point, all I did was put my head on the pillow so I could sleep.

I recalled waking up and seeing my daughter peeking at me to see if I was still home. She was happy just to see my feet or legs at the edge of the bed. That was good enough to let her know her mom was still at home, and even though I made bad decisions in my life, me and my daughter had a closeness like no other. I always made sure I talked to her about school, boys, and especially the streets. I knew my daughter adored me, and she never wanted for anything, believe it or not. I love Samone with all my heart, soul, and mind. I just did not love myself. And I was more upset with myself that I failed again. She was about sick of me at this point, not to mention heartbroken.

*Oh boy. Here I go thinking again about my past.*

I just forgot I was in here for this warrant. They still hadn't given me a roommate. I started to yell out of my cell. "Hey, when do I go to court?" They screamed at me. "Davis, shut up, and you better be happy the police didn't find that gun at your mother's house. You go to court on your bench warrant in the morning!" I've been sitting here in this stinky cell for over six hours, and I've managed to think of the most terrible things I've done in my life, but being in jail this time was so different.

As I sat on the hard bed, I started to feel funny. All I was thinking about all of a sudden was how disappointed my daughter was. I remembered the look on her face as if she was in this cell with me. I began to cry. I realized how much of a failure I've been. I cried so much within that hour the pillow was soaked.

Then all of a sudden I started to feel this tremendous presence in my cell and had enough sense to know that if I was going to get a prayer through, this would be the time. So I got on my knees, and I cried out to the Lord and told Him how ridiculous and pitiful I've become—how people were always talking about me in and out of the neighborhood, how I know He's not pleased with my lifestyle, how sorry I was for putting so much worry on my poor mother, how I have disrespected my body how I disappointed my daughter, but most of all how I disrespected Him.

I felt the Lord put His arms around me and told me how much He loved me no matter what I've done in the past, and I was thinking to myself, *But, Lord, it was just yesterday!* He told me, "Camille, I love you. I loved you when you didn't love yourself. Your daughter will be fifteen this year. If you don't get yourself together, you'll lose her to the streets. How many days and years are you going to destroy your life? You really don't like yourself, Camille, but if you put your trust in me, I can remove all that is wrong with you.

"With me, you can handle the guilt and shame of your past. Don't you know I was with you when you walked into dark hallways to get drugs? Don't you know I was with you when people had pit bulls ready to charge at you? Don't you know I was with you when you stole a dope dealer's money and jewels, and he chased you out with a gun? Don't you know I was with you when you had the nerve to talk slick to people in taverns? Don't you know I was with you when young dope dealers wanted and plotted to take your life because you didn't pay them on time? I've been with you all this time, Camille. Your daughter, Samone, and your mother have been standing in the gap in prayer for you all this time. You're blessed to still have your mother here. You need to be a help to her not a hindrance. I want you to start doing what's right.

"Camille, you'll make mistakes along the way but repent quickly. Don't you know that was why I died on Calvary? I did it just for people like you. The cross means you're free from all sinful things, drugs, and any other corrupted lifestyle. Camille, you will never find love like you'll find in me. You need to believe in me when you don't feel me because I know your fears and I know your pain, and I'll be with you all the way. I am a friend to the friendless."

And it was then I realized God was my roommate. I started to thank Him for being with me in my cell when I was at my worst. I started to thank Him that my mother was still in the land of the living. I wanted to focus on God restoring my trust and relationship back with my daughter, so I continued to cry out and thank Him. I couldn't thank Him enough. I repented for everything I could think of.

Before I knew it, it was morning time. I didn't realize I prayed and cried with the Lord all that night. All of a sudden, the deputy spoke over the intercom and told me I had court that morning. So I stayed on my knees a little longer and asked God to come into my life and asked Him to remove anything necessary to avoid anything related to alternative and drug lifestyles and any other lifestyles that weren't pleasing to Him. When I got off my knees, I quickly brushed my teeth, combed my hair the best I could, and got ready for court. Then it dawned on me as I combed my hair and brushed my teeth how I could stare at myself in the mirror for the first time in a long while.

After court, they released me and dropped the bench warrant. But before I even got to my mother's house, the Lord already warned me that my mother wasn't going to let me stay. I know she was embarrassed and mad that the police came in to search her home for a gun. I was the last person she wanted to see at that moment. And sure enough, as soon as I knocked on the door, she let me in, but quickly told me, "Camille, you can't stay here. You're going to have to move." So I replied, "Okay, Mom, but will you just give me at least two weeks? And I promise to be gone." She said, "Alright," and I didn't leave the house in those two weeks unless it was church-related.

I quickly found a job and a place to stay and after staying clean for a couple of months I was walking to the store, and this woman witnessed me. She gave me a track with the beautiful name of a church: God's Glory. I went to the next Sunday, and the first lady of the church was like no other first lady I have ever met. She was so personal. She didn't mind crying while holding you and making you feel like she was your friend. You really don't find that kind of love with first ladies in the church because they are usually very stuffy. They were not even approachable. But this woman was the sweetest first lady I had ever met.

Everyone from the missionaries to the mothers in the church drew me in with so much love. Then her husband entered on his way to the pulpit. You could tell he had so much authority. When that man preached, I knew at that very moment this is my church. He was funny, encouraging, and powerful. When you leave, you know you have a good church.

One morning, the pastor got on the subject of homosexuality, and the *truthful* sermon almost made me jump right out of my seat. The Lord knew deep in my heart I really wanted a change so I stayed right there. His sermons made you want to be free from sin and not just one sin of all unrighteousness. And at the end of his sermon, he would shout out, "Who the Lord has set free is free indeed!" And I would be so excited because I finally had some hope for my future.

As I and my daughter sat in church, her eyes went from being hurt by my drug lifestyle to admiration as she would look at me in the corner of her eyes. I started to see a young teenager who praised the Lord even harder. Our mother-and-daughter bond got stronger, and we were so happy. Our church always prayed, read, and fasted three days a week, and I found myself getting stronger and stronger until I realized I'd been sober and clean from everything for three years, from 2007 until 2010. I was so excited. I remembered what Cheryl Wilks from the *house of corrections* told me. She said if I was clean for one year, I could go with her and give my testimony at the *jails*.

Walking in that place for the first time and not being a prisoner made me feel so powerful, and my daughter could not have been so happy and proud of her mother. I was so proud of myself that I decided to tell my pastor, and his reply I did not like. He told me he did not think it was time for me to be doing prison ministry yet. I thought he was jealous or he didn't want me to succeed in ministry. Even though I still went to prison to give my testimony, it wasn't long before things started to change for me.

Before May of 2010, all of a sudden, I just started drinking. I've been sober for three years, I had a new truck, and everything spiritually and materially was good, but all the trust I built up with my daughter and my mother went right out the window. I almost thought I heard *Satan* laughing at me. It was terrible not only for me, and the disappointment of my daughter hurt me the most.

A couple of years later Cheryl Wilks passed away. All I could think about was how this woman helped me get on the right track and how proud I was of myself for being able to go back into the prison ministry how disappointed she had to be that I returned to the same mess, but mostly I couldn't stand myself so instead of sobering up, I drank more and started smoking crack again. My missions got worse. There were knives being put to my neck, guns drawn, and dope dealers lying telling me I gave them fake $100 bills just to get another one. I would cry and run back to the altar every chance I got, but I knew I lost the anointing the Lord had given me, and I was powerless. And it will only take one person or any situation just to make me mad so I could drink and get high.

I started to realize my daughter was always nervous, and I knew I was to blame. Guns going off in the neighborhood, I'm sure she wondered if I got shot. Even though I got her everything she needed, she wanted me to be home and me to be a mother, and even though she was in good hands, I'm sure she got tired of being just with her grandmother and me not home.

Me not being there made her insecure, angry, and embarrassed, not to mention very hurt. *Women, you need to realize how much our children grieve when we're not at home with them, especially when the children know it's drug related.* They actually start to question themselves as if they are the problem. My dumb butt thought I was alright because I talked to her about the streets, boys, and having good grades. But my daughter saw her mother running in and out of the home for years and just coming home to find out I lost my job or I got in a car accident, or I was in jail, or something negative. But one thing I must say about my Samone was that she turned out like *a young queen.* I said that because I never met anyone like her in my life.

It was beneath my daughter to engage in conversation if someone was being talked about. She hated cursing and did not place herself in any messy or *ungodly* situations and didn't like anyone to draw negative attention to her. She does not like fake and unnecessary compliments because she's not a vain person. She's a tactful young lady who stays quiet and always has a humble spirit—very sensitive but strong-willed. I'm sure kids would see me and tell her, "Your mother's on crack," or "Your mother's a dyke," and I can't imagine the pain I'm sure it caused. But she still showed me so much love because children are so forgiving, and I believe she was just happy to see me and know I was alive.

I was not saying she didn't get angry because there were times when she would yell, "Who do you think you are, Mom? You think you can just come home, and everything will go right back to being normal again? Well, Mom, I'm mad at you. You're so selfish I don't even want to look at you. You make me sick!" Then my butt would say, "You're right." I have nothing to say but "You're right." And then I would go upstairs like a child.

I wanted to blame everybody else, my pastor, my mother, just anybody but me, and when I talked about my pastor, it wasn't long before I got into a car accident. My vehicle rolled over twice, and I walked away. Thank the Lord. But I realized you shouldn't talk about any pastor especially if it wasn't his fault. I was blessed to still be alive but realized why the accident happened. *You shouldn't ever talk about a pastor.* They put me in jail, and I got right out.

Throughout those months, I was in and out of the church, and saints would ask my daughter, "How's your mother?" She would smile and simply say, "She's fine. Just pray for her." She never ever busted me out even though the saints weren't stupid. They knew my crackhead butt went right back out there. My daughter stayed true to me trusting in the Lord with hopeful eyes and a grieving spirit and knowing in her heart God would one day answer her request concerning me.

When I got out after the car accident, I didn't even come home right away. I had money in my account so I went out drinking even though I was in great pain. I didn't go home for two days. When I finally got home, I pounded hard on the front door. My mother just opened the door and let my funky butt in, and I passed by my daughter, and her arms were crossed like a parent's arms out of disgust, so I just went to my room and slept it off, then went right back out there and started drinking again. I would get everything my daughter needed and give my mother money and tell them, "I'll be back," and be gone.

One evening as I was drinking, I ended up on Twenty-seventh Street close to Walnut Avenue. I had been there for a while. There were mostly the same people, but as I was smoking, all my attention was on the crack I had on the table. There was a young lady who had been at the table for days just like me, but we never really talked much. I remembered she was just looking at me strangely all day. Then out of nowhere, *all of a sudden*, she told me how I gave my testimony to prisoners at the *house of correction,* and all I could do was hold the hot pipe in my hand. I was in shock. I could not believe someone whom I witnessed to was actually there at a crack house where I was sitting at, smoking. *Damn!*

The rock that I put on the hot pipe sizzled away, and the crackhead next to me just grabbed my pipe and started smoking what I put on it. I couldn't say anything. I felt like dropping dead. I was the living dead, and at that very moment, I felt so disgraced and embarrassed, and she even made it worse by having a smirk. It was as if Satan himself was staring me right in my face saying, "You have been exposed, dummy!" I couldn't even get high anymore. There were no words to tell you how bad I was feeling if there was a word to express I couldn't. All I wanted to do was get as far away as I could.

As I left, I just shook my head back and forth out of disgust. I just wanted to disappear. Nothing was going right at that time, and God was trying to get my attention. Other things started to happen to me: people just trying to set me up, people putting mickeys in my drinks trying to put me to sleep. The Lord said in His sweet voice, "Don't you know *Satan* wants to kill you?" All I could do was cry because I felt so lousy, so ashamed, so embarrassed. My reputation became more terrible. People hated to see me coming and were glad to see me going.

And before I knew anything, it was already 2012, and I was still struggling. The Lord even allowed me to perform my poetry on television, and in local churches. I even formed The Davis Theatrical Poetry Group, with my daughter and niece, and we performed at Great Faith Miss. Baptist Church, and when we finished the great late

Pastor Nabors looked at me and told me to keep writing. That was something I will always cherish and hold dear to my heart.

Even though God opened up doors for me to do my ministry, I still messed up. I lay in my bed and talked with the Lord. I said, "God, I can't seem to do anything right. I'm not right. I don't know how to be right. Lord, I don't even trust myself, so I'm not even going to make you any more promises, because I can't keep them. I hate the way I look. I'm overweight. In my mind, I still want to be with women, even though the sexual act is done. In my mind, Lord, I still desire them." I started to realize I wasn't happy and felt empty and out of place. I believed in the word, and in the word, I know I could not make it to the gates of *heaven* sleeping with women.

This depression went on for months until out of nowhere God's sweet voice said to me, "Camille, I know you can't do it. You can't do anything without me. I want you to love me and build a relationship with me. Let me be your mate." He even told me that when I want to drink and get high. I don't even try hard enough to fight, that I didn't want it bad enough so how could He help a person like me, and that it wasn't my fault that I had a low opinion of myself as a young teenager, and it wasn't my doing but I needed to forgive the family member that made me feel like the bottom of my shoe.

Jesus told me that I am very special to Him in every way. He even told me He love me because I wasn't ashamed to praise Him anywhere. How happy He was when I would clap my hands and cry out to Him. *Satan* tried to make me feel stupid going to the altar every Sunday, but I knew God honored it. God knew I was hurting and very godly sorry for all the shameful things I had done in my life. He started to remind me of how many times He saved my life, and I didn't even know it.

*Jesus* told me I've been at death's door many times, and even though my sins *stunk heavy in his nostrils*, He never let anyone or anything touch me to the point where it took my *life*. The Lord told me how I was still doing the same stupid old things and how I'd become more ratchet than ever, that I looked ridiculous hanging out all hours of the night on Villard Avenue with my old self as if I was homeless, stealing dumb things like government cell phones and $20 here and there, going in people's pants pockets quickly after seeing them go to the time machine, and straight-up just ripping them completely off. The last *crack house* I was in was full of mentally ill people, including myself, because I stayed too long.

*Jesus* told me about the craziness in that particular spot. The schizophrenic behavior that was there, and I knew it and still stayed. There were arguing, knives being drawn, and a lot of mental reactions. All this behavior at one time and the house was crowded, anyone could have been killed at any moment. The Lord went on and began to tell me there were *spirits* in that house that could have actually sent my mental state completely over the edge, and it wouldn't have too much. He said, "I've been warning you for years. *Take heed of My mercy. Take heed of My grace. You are going to die in sin if you don't take listen, Camille!*"

I knew I needed to stop beating myself up. I needed to stop being on the pity pot, always a victim, being mad all the time, and setting myself up for failure. Even though

I had a very low opinion of myself, I had enough sense to know the root was planted when I was young. And on my journey of thoughts, there had been more than one person in my family who hurt me. It was hard for me to forgive because the hurt was so great. It was easier to just drink the pain away even though I knew it would destroy me. I knew Satan tricked me out of a healthy life.

When I became an adult, I was very angry and had a lot of hatred. My view of men was totally destroyed. I knew the Lord was doing something with me because being around attractive women became uneasy. I couldn't really ever be too comfortable in my relationships because of my Christian beliefs. Yes, I would be with them, but always in the back of my mind, I believed God wasn't pleased, so I became very uncomfortable.

As the years rolled by, I got numb to my beliefs and continued in sin until one evening I was in the bed with this woman, and I couldn't engage in any sexual act. It was as if Jesus was in the room. All I can tell you was I felt His presence strongly, and I got up from the bed. She wondered what was wrong, and when I told her, she got mad and talked about how God loves everyone. She even went on to say we were born this way and that we would go to heaven. But I told her God doesn't make anything that will send you to hell.

I continued to tell her I believe in all of the Bible, not just the sections that just make me feel happy. *I believe it's an abomination.* And I went on to tell her how this lifestyle made me feel uncomfortable. That we will not inherit the kingdom of God. The Bible says it in 1 Corinthians 6:9. Then I told her that in verse 11, it says, "And such were some of you: but ye are washed, but ye are sanctified, but ye are justified in the name of the Lord Jesus, and by the spirit of our God." In other words, God was saying He could change us. That such *were* some of us. We could actually change. That He would *wash* us with spiritual cleansing. And that He would *sanctify* us which means He'll set us apart, meaning we'll even start looking saved and spiritually different. People will know we've changed. And then He says He'll *justify* us, which means people who bring up our past were justified because of the *blood He shed on the cross.* By the time I got done talking to her, we separated in the house and I yelled, "Whose report will I believe? I will believe in the report of the Lord" (Isaiah 53:1). And as the months rolled by, we parted ways. But even though I stopped messing around, it didn't stop people from talking about me. And to be honest I still feel the same in my heart. God had me thinking more on a deeper level on how others made me feel concerning my sexuality. People yelled those very same verses to me and Bible bashed me almost to death trying to make me feel shameful. Then I had to think about what scriptures were they hiding behind. All I know is I'm going to concentrate on Matthew 7: Do not judge. Only God can judge us. Not to mention people acting as if we shouldn't be in churches as if God doesn't love us. That's why he shed his blood. The church is not only for praise and worship, but it's a hospital for the lost and sick people that are in despair. People should stop spectating, turning their noses down at folks, and concentrate on getting their own break through asking the Lord to forgive them for what they are hiding behind closed doors.

Things didn't change. I just stopped sleeping with women. I didn't get too upset when folks talked because they had good reason. But it made me medicate myself more. I realized I didn't keep myself unspotted from the world like what is said in James 1:27. So that's to be expected. I had to stop and give up everything, surrender everything to God, and allow Him, not man, to heal my hurt. I had to learn how to cry out to the Lord and stop reacting to anything and everyone that bothered me. I needed to put my trust in Him even when it looked bad.

Even though people were still talking about me, I needed to remind myself of the book of Psalms Chapter 3. When people said there was no help for me in God, *He'll* smite all my *enemies* on the cheekbone, *He* will let me sleep, and then *He* will wake me up and *sustain* me. He told me not to be afraid of tens of thousands of people who have set themselves against me roundabout. *How He's my glory the lifter up of my head.* When I meditated on those verses, I can make it.

At the end of 2012, my mother told me her doctor diagnosed her with dementia. When she told me, it hurt me so bad I cried for days because she was scared, and I didn't want to believe it, but I stayed strong when I spoke to her about the power of God. Before the end of that same year, she came to me and asked me if I would be her caretaker. I quickly accepted and was honored. She said, "Camille, I want you to be my caretaker, upon my death I want you to have the house Camille and I want Dexter (my brother) to handle my finances." So I called my brother to come over, and she told him what she wanted. In my heart, I felt if she passed away, he wouldn't honor it, so I asked my mother if she would be willing to make a will concerning me getting the home upon her death. She quickly said yes, so we went to Allan Silverstein, and I paid for the will while she was still a component.

For three and a half years, I did so great taking good care of her going to work every day, we were going to church every Sunday, my mother and I were very happy. I was so proud of myself for not using when I go to work every day until I noticed that my mother's condition got just a little worse, and I needed more help, but the family was living their lives and were too busy. I was welding for western products and had to take a leave of absence due to no family help until a year later I messed up. When my mother would fall asleep, I would sneak off to my friend's home on the same block and come home later and later, until one time, she wasn't home when I got there. So I called my niece, and she told me my mother was with her.

After a day or so, she missed me and came back home. I felt so terrible that I got myself back on track. But four months later, the same thing happened, and she ended up at my brother's, but he couldn't take it. My mother drove him crazy because he couldn't handle her illness. I called my best friend, Daphne. I cried to her about not getting any help from my family, that my family should have stepped in a long time ago, seeing that I kept relapsing off and on— that it was a cry for help. But when I thought about it, it seemed like they wanted me to fail. The next day or so, I got a call from my daughter. She said, "Nana misses you so much," and that made me so happy. I quickly rushed over to my brothers and took her back home.

After that, the state helped me with other caretakers so I could go back to work. My friend down the block was even willing to help, and he watched her for a few weeks. I know my mother was glad to be in her home and glad to see me. Every time I would come home from work, she would be so happy. She would say, "Camille, there you are. I love you." And I would say, "Mom, I love you too." I remember the times when I always made sure the front and back doors were secured so if I took a bath or was cooking or washing clothes, she couldn't just walk out, and she would get so mad at me. One day she tried to leave the house, and when she saw she couldn't, she said, "What the hell is this mess?" Sometimes she would become combative and hit me and tell me to get out of her house.

Sometimes when family friends would come by the house, she'd tell them undercover as if she was being mistreated. But I knew she didn't understand what was going on and that things started becoming confusing to her. When I look back, it was kind of funny because every few minutes, she'd say, "Camille, I'm sorry, but what's going on?" and I had to say "Mom, I need to be with you if you go outside, and you need to put on some shoes." She just didn't understand why she just couldn't walk out like she used to. Within that same year, the state stayed in our face because family members were making accusations concerning her safety but when they came over, they couldn't find fault. Life became so stressful. The only vice I came to was drinking again.

Some family members were quick to criticize but not willing to help. During the fifth year of my mother's illness, things went tough. Soon my daughter will be leaving to go to college. She's going to Stevens Point University to get her bachelor's degree, in social services. It was such an emotional time because I knew she wouldn't be home anymore, and there was a heaviness like never before. There was a lump continually in my throat and deep in my heart. It seemed like things went too fast in my mind. I was saying to myself, "Did you tell her everything she needs to know?" It was like I was losing a child to death. I had such a sick feeling, but I was happy for her because she was doing something to add purpose to her life.

After I went there to send her off in a couple of hours, it was time for me to come back to Milwaukee. Soon my Greyhound bus will be pulling up, and it will be time to say our goodbyes. As the bus rolled up, my daughter grabbed me tight, kissed me all over my face, and told me she loves me, and with the biggest tears I've ever seen on her face, I started to cry. As we hold each other while rocking back and forth, she kept telling me how much she loves me and how wonderful of a mother I really was. And as the bus doors closed, she passed me one of the most heartfelt letters I have ever read.

She wrote how she was proud of me, how I taught her a lot and how she never wanted for anything, how I was there when it counted the most, how much she loves me, how she'll miss me and the times when we laugh and watch certain movies, and how I put the drugs down when she had a real problem. She said more, but I was just happy to hear that. And on my way back to Milwaukee, I had four hours to think about my life and what I needed to do now that she was gone.

As the years rolled on, I was still taking care of my sweet mother the best I can, and I realized caretaking can be very stressful especially when the caregivers were not even showing up, and the family was still too busy to help. I've become very angry because the only time my family got my mother was when I messed up. I felt like we all should have taken turns. It was all placed on me.

It's now 2017, and my mother was placed with a family member because of my negligence. I allowed this disease to hijack my brain, and my ass didn't come home after work and left my mother with the TempsPlus caretakers, and it forced the state to place her with my niece. *I fucked up.* I let my addiction get the best of me. My life was now the darkest it's ever been, and all I want to do was *scream*. All I can think of was how my mother wanted to be in her own home. I knew my mother was miserable and missed me. I remembered going over to my niece to visit my mother and how she would pull on my sleeve, and I knew she wanted to come home, but I had already messed that up. I felt like *shit*! So I tried to make sure I would see her as much as possible.

As the months rolled by, my mom started sleeping a lot more, and I noticed things were different because her dementia had progressed, and she wasn't the same joyful smiling Marguerite. Her loss of memory got worse. As I reached to hold her in my arms, I felt complete sadness because I was the cause of all this shit. One Sunday, I wanted to take my mother to the new church we joined that was at the corner of our street. The name of our church was St. Emmanuel's, and when I got there, she was ready, so we walked to the church like we normally did. But my mother was so frail, and her breathing was very shallow.

Within two hours, after my mother got home from church, my niece called me and told me my mother had been admitted to the hospital. Within that week she was in hospice. I stayed at the nursing home around the clock. *You couldn't pay me to leave.* I would go to work during the night, and my mother would see my face in the morning. My mother would be sitting in a wheelchair with the other patients, and I remembered the sad look on her face, which hurt me to my heart. I knew she didn't want to be there. Edema developed in her legs, not to mention she was heartbroken just knowing she was there.

One evening at dinner, I swear she gave me a look of disappointment, and that was when I knew she knew where she was. My mother's wish was to be in her home. I feel knowing where she was made her dementia and state of mind worse. It angered me that the nurses didn't attend to changing her bottom and cleaning her. I noticed her bottom was raw, and I became very enraged. The night shift didn't attend to her, so I had the supervisors take pictures of her bottom, and they knew I was there, and I was aware not to mention upset so I started changing her myself. In my mind, all I could think was, *My poor mother I could just cry.*

The following week I was told all they could do was give my mother morphine and that I couldn't give her water or anything to eat. When I heard that, I stopped going to work and stayed with my mother around the clock. As the nights went by, I remembered praying next to her asking God to forgive me and asking my mom to forgive me. I remembered laying my head on her lap as I knelt down on my knees whimpering with one arm holding her waist telling her how much I loved her and how sorry I was for not coming home that last time. I cried and told God and my mother how sorry I was that I messed up and how sorry I was that she was not in her home like she wished. I remember crying all that night until I fell asleep on the floor next to her.

When I woke up, I realized the caretaker who was assigned to her room never even came in to change her, so I snapped and I changed her but told them to still do their *damn* job. Later that morning, the state nurse came and told us that my mother didn't have a pulse. So my sister-in-law stated that day would probably be the day that she'll die. But I didn't try to hear it. The day went on, and my niece Janel came in. While laughing and talking, my family friend looked at me and said, "Camille, I want you to tell your mother you're going to be alright so she doesn't worry about you." My niece Janel and I sat looking at Mom, then all of a sudden the hospice nurse said, "Camille, your mother is trying to talk."

I looked at my mother, and she was moving her head trying to tell me something. Before we knew anything, my daughter Samone and her son's father walked into the room. Then my mother mumbled to me, "Camille, I love you," and she said it again, and all I could say is, "Mom, I love you," and I quickly remembered what my family friend told me to tell her. I told her, "Mom, don't worry about me. I'm going to be alright." I continued to tell her to go with God to go unto His bosom, and that was when she took her last breath, and she was gone.

She left me. She died, and all we could do was cry. It was the most devastating event in my entire life. I have no life, I didn't know what to do, and I was in a state of total confusion. I didn't expect her to just go that quick. I needed more time. God, I didn't expect that would be her last breath. I was so *hurt* that I couldn't feel. I couldn't sleep. My mind was consumed and focused only on her last breath. I was in such a state of shock but happy to know my mom wasn't alone. My mother was *aware, knowingly* seeing me, *hearing* me at that very moment, and her two granddaughters, Samone and Janel. We were *blessed*.

My mother saw my first breath, and God allowed me to see her last breath. I sat there by her side on her death-bed, and I thank God for giving me that comfort, that greatness, that honor. Had I not been there for that last breath, it would have killed me. I had enough guilt, so God knew I needed that and I thank Him. Golden Gate Funeral Parlor took my mother's body. And the next day, my two nieces, my sister-in-law, and I banded together to make the funeral arrangements. My brother and I had already started her burial funds before she died. But we had $2,000 more to go, so my two nieces had the responsibility of putting up the rest of the money.

At the time of the actual funeral, I was very disappointed because my sister-in-law actually was bragging about her nephew. She told me, "My nephew is in the ministry of music." So of course I said, "Great. We had it all figured out." Janel put in $1,000 for the burial and did the obituaries. Bianca ordered my mother's dress from New York and put $1,000 for the burial. The next day, I prepared for the funeral, and my niece Janel wanted to go into one of the closest in my mother's house to make a collage, and as I and both my nieces were going through different things in boxes, we found all the money my mother saved during most of our lifetime, enough for Bianca and Janel to get the money back they put into the burial and enough for me to clear back taxes on the house.

The money people accused me of stealing from my mother during the time I took care of her we had found in a tied-up stocking. At the time of the actual funeral, my sister-in-law, as I mentioned, was supposed to be in charge of the music. But as the funeral went on, it was more like a *damn* church service, just regular singing. I was *livid*. It took all of me just not to snap. Before the funeral, we were all communicating, so how come she just couldn't say, "Camille, my nephew can't make it," so I could find someone else.

Hell, I could have found a known crackhead whom I knew could sing on Villard Avenue by the open pantry and cleaned her or him up good because my mother told me she wanted a home going which means good singing songs that make you cry. Mom stated to me that she wanted us to cry (LOL). Instead, I was mad as hell and uttered a few comments to which my niece Bianca turned her head and told me to be nice. So I just kept my mouth shut but it was hard. I was so upset that I did not dare even go up to make any remarks because there would have been some angry sarcastic words spoken. So I stayed seated.

And after the funeral, we buried her, and I said my goodbyes deep in my heart, got into the limousine, and went straight home. Of course, I partied hard, and I drank for two days straight. When I finally got home, my life wasn't the same. Something was missing, not just my mother. It was as if I was out of my element. Everything seemed to be in slow motion. It was like a badass nightmare. I felt uncomfortable like never before. I felt if I don't get a hold of myself, I could actually lose the rest of my mind. My heart was so broken to where I felt like King Kong because the hurt was so devastating. Nothing and nobody could match that. I was able to take anything after that trauma.

The house will never be the same; even drinking or inviting others over was crazy. I didn't realize until later when my mother's spirit ran people away. I'd be partying with people, and everyone who came to kick it with me would be in one room but staring through the living room as if they kept seeing something. So when they would take a hit, they'd actually run out of the dam house. These were people I knew who never acted like that when they got high. People would come over, and every one of them always acted as if they were looking at something in the living room. That was when I had to ask, "What's wrong with you?" and they would just stare. They were very uncomfortable. Then it dawned on me that my mother wanted them gone, and she was very successful at it.

This went on for a good year until I got tired of being so miserable I couldn't even get high anymore, and when I looked in the mirror, I drank and used myself elderly it seemed. I looked old to myself, and I told myself I couldn't go out like this. And my daughter wasn't letting me have my grandson which hurt me like hell. So I got into the Meta House for women. I was happy as hell to get out of the home I created a monster in.

The monster became filled with sadness, doom, and gloom because I allowed so many unhealthy folks in my home. The inside of my house was filled with all kinds of crazy spirits. But the spirit that latched on to me the heaviest was the spirit of fear. And I couldn't shake it for anything. I tried to pray my way out but knew I needed to leave my own crib. I needed to clear my mind in order to function. I had to get a new connection with myself but most of all my higher power.

I needed to start fresh because the Bible says not to dwell with unhealthy spirits, and I became the unhealthiest spirit of all. I couldn't believe the home my mother continually prayed and praised the Lord in and the home where friends and family could fall asleep became a home of havoc, and it was all my fault. So inpatient looked really good to me right now.

When I arrived, I actually felt like I was at a retreat (in my mind, anything beat the house of hell). I was told who my therapist was, but I really didn't know how tough she was going to be. She was strict. She didn't beat around the bush. She gave it to you straight from the hip. She was hard but knew how to soften it up and would use a bit of humor to a hard-headed person like myself so I could accept and own up to my bull shit. She would imitate me just like my mother would; she talked about how impatient I was and imitated my gestures to the point that all I could do was laugh at myself. I laughed so hard my stomach hurt. She was smart enough to get me to take a good look at me. And I realized I looked like an idiot. I couldn't get upset because it was so funny; it was as if my mother was imitating me herself, so not only did I know it was true, but it also made me aware of how others viewed me.

That was when it all came to me. I knew my mother played a big part in my recovery. And when I went back to my room, I cried out to God thanking Him for my therapist, Michele Williams. I haven't laughed like that in a long time, and I enjoyed spending time with her because it was like spending time with my mother. So I know this was where I needed to be, not to mention she was becoming the sister I always wanted. Focusing on my program, I learned a lot about myself and wanted more insight into why I was so f—— up! So my counselor suggested I see an outside therapist.

Upon meeting my outside therapist at SAQH Behavioral Health, I had a chance to discuss my shame and guilt concerning my mother. I revealed how I took care of her by myself without help from family and how stressful it became and how difficult some family members made it for me getting the state involved. But not willing to help. I remember crying to him sobbing tremendously. I confessed to the doctor about how I never returned on payday after work which removed my mother permanently. I cried so damn hard he had to stop me. He went on to tell me that my family wanted me to mess up for whatever reason, and the only thing I had was alcohol. That was all I knew at the time. That was my only stress reliever.

He went on to say I was already an abused child coming up because of the name-calling and the harsh words from that family member who hurt me terribly and that I never healed from that alone. Being called stupid, dumb, knucklehead, an idiot by that one family member all the time broke my spirit a long time ago. Not to mention that family member probably had the same treatment growing up as well. And since my father was an alcoholic and my mother had depression, I was a candidate for disaster. He said I shouldn't feel terrible because I did the best I could for those eight years. He also told me to stop believing people when they talk about my impulsive manner because I've had trauma.

He told me my hyper reactions came from situational depression, that it was a response to something. Once the situation is solved, my depression would go away like any other person's. My reaction was energetic and hypervisualized, and it had a heightened sterol response because I was always waiting for the other shoe to drop, which was normal for a person who had never addressed past trauma. He was speculating it may have come from the murder of my sister Cozette. He reminded me in my conversation how I mentioned that my mother throughout all those years never stopped telling me, "Camille, I love you." That's one thing my mother never stopped saying because even she knew I was doing and taking care of her the best I could, not to mention how she adored me.

After that emotional session, I was so relieved. I got back to Meta House and began sessions with a new therapist. Her name was Danielle Armstrong, and she specialized in a therapy called EMDR. Now, this therapy was deep. In the very beginning, I almost got very angry because she kept rehashing the trauma and the guilt related to my mother by not coming home after work and leaving her with the TempsPlus care worker.

Focusing on her hand movements (one hand moving back and forth) was almost hypnotizing and could put you in a trance; while you're still alert. She'll have you focus on something beautiful in your mind so when you feel that trauma during your therapy, you can use that for your safe place mentally. (My safe place was me and my grandson at the beach in my mind). You had to have a comforting safe place in your mind during this type of therapy because it could become very dangerous. So it had to be done properly.

Getting there mentally was very emotional for me. Danielle started speaking about the things I shared with her concerning my mom, and things got pretty heated in my mind. I could actually smell cigarettes while visualizing arguing with certain family members. Different perfumes, I even thought I heard my mother's voice in my therapist's office during our session. It took a few sessions and after the fourth one, I started to believe in this EMDR. I did everything Danielle told me to do. I believed in her and wanted to heal badly from all my trauma. But the real test came when I got out of treatment.

Thanksgiving rolled around, and as usual, my big sister and I got into a little argument, and she made comments that would of course make me feel like crap. But this time I turned my head towards her and said, "My therapist told me you were gonna do this." And I walked out and went home. I'm thankful I had gone through that type of therapy, which I choose to call Christian EMDR. It prepared me not to react in an argumentative way. And after I went home it also prepared me not to beat myself up because of the comment she made.

The next day or so I got a text from my big sister telling me she was sorry, and to me, that was *big* because she rarely apologized; she was a person who'll say what she's got to say and keep it moving. But this time she begged my pardon, and I felt the apology through her text. I quickly accepted it and invited her to dinner that Christmas, but I got no reply. I just thought she'd get to it later. The day after Christmas I got a screaming phone call from her daughter yelling, "Auntie Camille, I'm at my mom's house and found my mom under her bed. She's dead!" All I could do was *scream.* My heart fell to the ground.

Out of all the deaths I've witnessed, I can honestly say I have sorrow in the pit of my heart that never went away. I was extremely hurt by this death. All this damn time I had wasted arguing and fighting with her when I should have just focused on forgiveness and trying to be closer to her. Chauncey meant the world to me; she taught me a lot. She was a great listener and always reminded me nobody owes me anything just because I spend all my money on them. She would say, "No one told you to spend all your money!" Boy was that a lesson.

At this point, I would have done anything to wipe the corner of her mouth while she eats. LOL. I would have done anything to watch her spill her big cup of milk. I would have gladly wiped it up for her. I would have loved to hear her sing in her odd tone of voice. I would have joined in just to hear her tell me to be quiet because now I messed her song up. LOL. I'll do anything to have her with me again.

Since then, it had been nothing but a blur. I really went in as far as all the drinking and drug use until September

3, 2021. I wanted to go back into treatment. After my sister Chauncey died in December of 2020, I started drinking again in September of 2021. I went for treatment at 2nd Century House for women, inpatient care. I was not doing anything good with my life. I had to get back into a healthy environment. That was my eleventh treatment. I didn't even know. I lost count. But I could say I was here for me, and not because I was running from some dope dealer because I owe him money. Or because my daughter's upset, and I couldn't see my grandson, or because I was under the influence. I've become an embarrassment again. I was here because I needed my life in order.

For the very first time, I can say I was really tired of my ass. At the rate I was going, I didn't have long. I felt my age. This life I was living is a pitiful one. It was sad to see myself. When I was young I wanted to be a police officer, a poet, and a writer, and I wanted to be in theaters, but being a lesbian and drug addict was not on my list. My drinking had become disrespectful, and I've developed an alter ego, one that was very rude and belittling. I can see someone was actually hurting me, simply taking me out. I've become Dr. Jekyll and Mrs. Hyde. I talk sarcastically way too much, and it was only by the grace of God I was still here. It was not my craftiness; it was God's.

Finally coming to my senses, I started to thank God and told Him how sorry I was and how I needed to address that little girl inside me who was confused about her sexuality, the little girl who still wet her bed as an adult. Professionals told me it's psychological. Nine times out of ten, it's related to my name-calling as a young child. None of these things was my fault. I gave myself permission to heal, to tell myself sorry, to stop destroying my life for things I had no control, to stop being so damn hard on myself. That's why I've been repeating all these negative behaviors. I can't help who I've become, all I can do was be better. Condemnation came from Satan, not God.

After reading John 3:17, I realized God never sent His Son to make us feel bad. He knew our struggles when He sent Jesus. But Satan had me focus on how I missed the mark. I found myself fighting for the love of God when He already loved me. He died for all the mess I struggled with. Now that's real love. God didn't expect me to change, only He can do that, even though there are going to be people who will never forget my past and even throw it in my face. This time I can smile because Romans 10:11 states, "Anyone who puts their trust in Him shall not be put to shame." So my mental health needed to be addressed.

You can't do all those drugs and all that kind of drinking for years and think things are going to go smoothly. I want to be a calm person in life when others say anything negative or when problems arise. I'll just inhale and exhale, take a hot bubble bath, and go to the lakefront to watch the waves, anything but snap. I don't have to explain or fight and argue anymore. I'll let God handle everything. I'm a grandmother now, and I want to see my grandson grow up, and I want to develop a healthy bond with him. That would mean the world to me. He loves his granny. And the love I feel for him is like no other. He's charming, adorable, handsome, funny, and smart. (What a joy).

I am so happy to finally be living a life I was proud of, but most of all a life my daughter was happy with; she can finally see her mother clean and sober but most of all acting like I got some damn sense. She so deserves this from me. Heck, I deserve it. Yes I know I am going to make some mistakes, but relapse will not be one of them. So I'll stay humble and aware, always constantly having my armor on at all times, because I can't go back to that thick pool of vomit. So I have a lot of work to do to stay grounded. Ten percent was the drugs, and 90 percent was me and my behavior so you know I got work to do because I'm a hot mess. LOL. All I can say is *greater is He who's in me than He who's in the world. I can do all things through Christ who strengthens me.* One more thing, I got two humble apologies, one from my niece and another from my daughter saying how sorry they were for not helping me more with my mother. *Wow.* To me that was *big.* It made me so happy.

# Acknowledgments

Thank you for your support. I would like to thank all the therapists, both in Meta House and 2nd Century House, for putting up with me.

I like to give special thanks to my daughter, Samone, and my grandson who helped keep me grounded.

Also, I give lots of love and thanks to my aunt Gertrude who always supported me no matter what and who always spoke loving and kind words of encouragement. For that, I'll always love and thank God for her.

To my beloved mother, Marguerite Davis; to my beloved father, Charles Davis; to my two beloved beautiful sisters, Chauncey and Cozette; my great friend and partner in life, Wendy; to my brother-in-law, Jimmy K.; Mr. SLAUGHTER; my best friend, Merle O.; my friend, Kalvin C., his nephews Lonny(Mann), and Brandon. My buddies Eddie Carter, Maryann Carter, James Phillips; and all the hosts of mothers who have helped me in my struggles such as Mrs. Margaret on Thirty-ninth, Erie Crowder, Mother Hurt, Pat Kohloff, Donald Tompson, G-Man, Minnie Henderson, Sister Cherly Wilkes, my Aunt Daisy, Dorothy, Sister Perterson, Mother Walker, Deacon and mother Gore, and Gloria Gore.

Also, a very special thanks to my Beloved Sister Chauncey who gave me my first typewriter in 2007. Which inspired me and that's when I really started writing thank you (I MISS YOU).

I would especially like to thank my two responsible nieces Bianca and Janal for being so supportive, loving me giving tuff love and always rescuing my crazy butt no matter what. Bianca is the matriarch of the family and Janal is the family hero who also was the first person. in the family to graduate from college setting a great example for my daughter Samone who we call the voice of reason. I know your mothers would be proud of how you two young women have turned out. I know as your auntie I am. Thank you to my niece Cydra who was a comfort and a blessing. How you were the only person that had enough sense to warmly wrap your arms around me at my mother's burial site while I grieved looking at my mother's casket. For that, you'll always hold a special place in my heart. To all my nephews who are in my corner always making their auntie laugh Kyle, James Sr. James Jr., Callum, Cayden, Devin, Ayden, his sister Amyah, Prentise and Derrick. Kalan, Dominick, Chantel, Giovanni, James (Stinky Man). I love you all with all my heart.

You can reach me at camilledavis443@gmail.com if you have any feedback or questions. With much love, Camille E. Davis.

MOTHER AND MY FATHER

MOTHER AND STEP FATHER, TERRY

My Brother Lyle Dexter

Sisters. Cozette and Chauncey

My Great Grandmother Lucy from Bloomington IL

My uncles Torrence and Homer from Bloomington IL

God Grandma pastor of Waukesha Temple Church

Wendy

My 1st friend, Mrs Crowder

Long time loyal friend Merle Orr

Mrs. Margaret from 39th

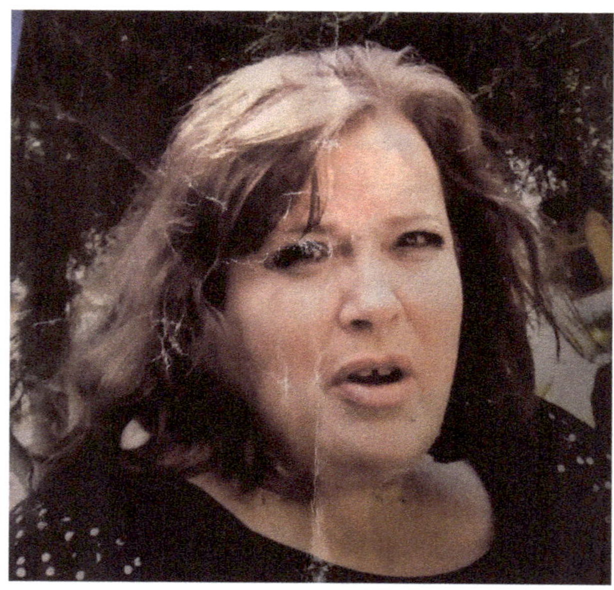

Sister Cheryl Wilkes from HOC

Me and my grandsons EMDR safe place

Bianca, Me and, Janel. My responsible niece's

My supportive daughter. SAMONE

My daughter Samone's Statement:

Early August of last year, I remember a woman who appeared so much different than what we all see today. This woman last year was consumed with her addiction, she was angry at the world, she was hurting, she didn't take care of herself, she was irresponsible, she was downright mean. I loved this woman as my mother but I disliked being around her for an extended length of time. And even though she was still there for me as a mother she was selfish at times. One year later, and I now see a woman who is strong, a woman who is able to fight temptation and cravings from a substance that once controlled her, a woman that prays, a woman that is able to save money and be responsible, a woman that walks with her head held high. A great mother and grandmother. She actually has my son more than I do and helps me tremendously. A woman that I actually enjoy being around now. Our relationship used to be filled with anger, hurt, and unforgiveness. And now it's filled with laughter, enjoyment and a mother daughter bond that is strong. We have a true friendship. I said all that just to say, that mom being proud of you is an understatement. You make recovery look so easy but I know there were days you struggled but the important thing is that you didn't pick up. You didn't give in. I would like to thank God who really answered my prayer concerning this. I would also like to thank everyone in her recovery program whether it was a director, peer or counselor who supported my mom through this journey. And lastly I would like to thank you mom because you did all the necessary steps to put the work in. I love you and I look forward to celebrating more years to come. Thank you.